A Prayer the Body Makes

A Prayer the Body Makes

Poems by

Penny Harter

Cover design by Shay Culligan

ISBN: 978-1-952326-04-2

Kelsay Books Inc.

kelsaybooks.com

502 S 1040 E, A119
American Fork, Utah 84003

Acknowledgments

Poems in this volume have appeared
in the following periodicals or anthologies:

Adanna: "The Solitary Birch," "Watersheds"

Alphabet Soup : "Marmalade"

The Crafty Poet II: "Dear Magnolia," "To Ride the Waves"

Hospital Drive: "When I Taught Her How to Tie Her Shoes,"
   "A New Beginning"

Jersey Shore Poets: "Darning Socks"

Naugatuk River Review: "My Father's Memory"

Persimmon Tree: "A Prayer the Body Makes"

Poetry Breakfast: "The Known Earth"

The Book of Donuts: "Valentine's Day at the Spousal Loss Support
   Group"

The Quotable: "Measuring the Distance"

Red Wolf Journal: "The Great North Woods"

The Practicing Poet: "Anniversary"

Tiferet: "Dream Hat"

Truck: "Shadow World"

Silver Birch Press: "Into the Lake"

Truck: "Hearing Voices"

Verse-Virtual: "Far," "Two Children on the Seaside Rocks,"
    "Tramps," "Honoring Angels," "Houses," "Remember Me,"
    "Listening to Furniture," "Breaking Morning,"
    "Seeing Familiar Faces," "Beyond the Mirror,"
    "They're Coming Back," "Across the Autumn Field,"
    "Butterfly Kisses," "Spring Blues,"
    "The Eastern Bluebird on Spring Grass,"
    "Darning Socks," "Healing the Wound With Honey,"
    "When I Taught Her How to Tie Her Shoes," "Running Wild,"
    "A Prayer the Body Makes," "Whose Newborn"

Visual Arts Collective: "Into the Lake," "Undone"

Your Daily Poem: "A Kind of Hunger"

Deep thanks to Virginia Center for the Creative Arts (VCCA) for a three-week residency in March 2015, during which I wrote a number of these poems.

Thanks, too, for inspiration found at Peter Murphy's annual Poetry and Prose Getaways in January 2015 and January 2017.

And special thanks to my poetry buddies Terry Ann Carter & Ce Rosenow, and my artist friend Anne Dushanko-Dobek, for their generous feedback on early drafts of some of these poems.

Contents

I

II

I

Hawk

When I see you, wings stretched wide
against the blue, sun threading your fringed
wingtips, my shoulders tense as if they could
sprout wings, as if I could rise to coast the
thermals with you, gliding over the sunset
field, weightless and free.

Shaping the air with my flight, I'd learn
the way of hawk, learn to savor a keen
vision that sees scrambling prey, learn
to hover, dive and eat, not minding feathers
in my beak, or bones. Perched on a fencepost,
I'd strip my prize clean.

Look, we say to one another, *there it is,
right there, just crossing the highway,
heading toward the ridge.* We crane our
necks, slow the car, roll down the window,
and already you have lifted us out of
ourselves, hawk, into your sky.

In last night's dream, I gathered up my
mother, small and easily draped over my
shoulder, to carry her off to some safe
haven. There was danger near us, maybe
flood or fire. And I woke before I knew
that she was whole.

Perhaps it was you I saved her from,
hawk, tiny creature that she was,
weaving her way through the tall grass
we all must brave on our path to sleep.
Or perhaps I *was* you, taking her back
to my ample nest, my little nestling.

Watersheds

At the Continental Divide, I should have been
a bird. Barely able to breathe in that rarified
air, I gave myself to range upon range of the
Rockies, my head spinning as I rose.

Once in a voiceless movie, shot from the
perspective of a hawk, I became both adult
and chick, flew high above the fields and
villages below, my wings rowing air.

Following the silver membrane of a river,
I traced its twists and turns through rosy hills,
cast my shadow on a thread of stream,
carried pungent wood-smoke home to nest.

The humans below me, what did they know
of the great water course? Did they feel the tug
of the moon on distant seas, the ebb and flow
of saline tides in mortal blood?

Yet back in my body, I remembered a dowser,
my late husband's grandmother, who, holding
a forked stick between her two gnarled hands,
almost lost her balance at the source.

Far

Distant or remote in time or space,
as in a far journey or distant music
on the wind. Beyond—a flickering
from the blue horizon.

Born into the longitude and latitude
of time, we emerge at a nexus of
shimmering lines. Remember those
old albums of black and white

glossies cornered into little black
pockets we licked and pasted onto
black pages? Fixed there, the faces
of our living and our dead stare at us

before they leap into the far, diving
over the edge. See how they shrink
to specks, draining the photograph
through an infinite funnel.

The shadow of a hawk just flew
across the springing grass. It, too,
comes from beyond, winging its way
toward tomorrow, tomorrow, and

tomorrow, in its wake a calendar
marked by bristle and bone, by fair
and fowl, as it arrows through the
aether of its wing-bound days.

Beyond the Windows

Here in this room we share, the future
is mute, will not announce its schedule of
intent. Glass shimmers between us and the
outside where a chill wind stirs the bare
limbs on budding trees. Open the window

to see the teacup you left on the picnic table
gathering stars all night now spill its light
into the dawn sky. Hear the robins trill across
the morning, *Come join with me, let's make*
a home and raise some more of us.

We trust blue eggs will fall into a sturdy nest,
then crack to free wet feathers and new beaks
gaping for more. Back in this room we share,
the furniture is mute. Ask the bed whose bodies
it will bear, or the dresser what garments will

echo tomorrow in its wooden drawers, and both
will answer you with dust. Beyond our window
other windows open into oceans of dark matter,
dark energy—those riddles we dangle bait for in
a sea whose waves break on our shifting shore.

Two Children on the Seaside Rocks

To paint the blue sky with storm clouds
threatening, or the foreground of rusty sea rocks
and pale water held between them, shimmering
with reflected sun—which did you choose first
as you set out the oils, stretched your canvas?

Or did you start by posing the two children
on the large boulder halfway out from shore,
their white aprons, soft blue jackets, and straw
hats catching the sun—the boy wearing
a faded tie, the girl with hand to mouth,

while you, perched farther out on the rocks
at low tide, easel precarious, strove to celebrate
that day, that place, and your children—possibly
my great-grandmother or great-grandfather—
solemnly staring at you through shaded eyes.

The rocks striated brown shot through with moss,
the weathered boathouse and dock at low tide,
the hazy garments blowing on the clothes line
strung between two trees behind the outhouse—
did you know, how could you know that you

were catching time in a sieve, netting the light
for me? How could you know that you were
stroking hope across a canvas, framing it in
gilt that shines across a century, inviting me
to sit with you that day in gratitude.

About Desire

One summer afternoon, lying face down in
the hammock strung between our magnolia
tree and a backyard maple, the child I was

thought she might dig all the way through
the Earth to China, then dive down the
tunnel she'd made and pop up from

the ground head-first, like a baby being
born or a bulb sprouting in early spring.
She did not wonder what soil she'd surprise,

what alien terrain would receive her—
only felt the need to find the other side
of now, the flip side of a waning day.

Memory is the box that holds desire,
starting in the amniotic womb—fetal
thumb pulsing in the nascent mouth.

The child I have again become
still wants to nurse on what might be,
still hungers for impossible rebirth.

Tramps

That's what they must have been,
or what we called them, we three
little girls roaming the woods that
began at the end of our neighborhood.

We knew those woods well—where
the skunk cabbage bloomed on its
island in the creek, or where tadpoles
lurked in the deeper woodland pools.

We were getting ready to vault that creek,
flying across on the rough poles we'd culled
from broken saplings, when we heard them
coming and soon saw them—three rough men

cutting through the underbrush and heading
toward the nearby gravel road. Young as
we were, something told us to hide behind
a hefty fallen trunk, duck our heads under

its branches heavy with their still green summer
leaves. Something told us to hold our breath,
to not move a muscle, to merge with the ferns
around our ankles, silent in flickering sunlight.

Those tramps passed so close beside us,
it seemed they must surely see us, might even
hurt us, though we did not fully understand
the kinds of hurt they might inflict.

Soon they were gone, but we stayed where
we were, each of us hidden like the roadside
fawn who by instinct crouches down among
tall grasses to be safe, to be safe, to be safe.

Dear Magnolia

How many days did I crouch beneath you on the damp
grass, collecting twigs and petals, shaping tiny people
and cloaking them in wilting hues of pink and rust?
A loner, I played more often by myself than with a friend,

stalking ants and beetles in the dust beneath the hedge.
Even now when magnolias flare in the yards I drive past,
creamy blossoms competing with Japanese cherry and
pear, I am back beneath you, combing the grass for clues.

If only I had not gone on a pilgrimage to the past, gone
to that remembered house my great-grandparents once
owned, hoping to see again my one true tree, or the ghost
of my young mother kneeling to weed the garden beds;

if only the new owners had not chopped you down, magnolia,
as they chose to expand and tar the once-pebbled driveway
until all I could find of you was a blacker circle on macadam—
a black hole still devouring our crumbling roots.

Ghost Garden

Once there were obedient rows prepared
for seeding annuals, and hardy perennials
dependable as the tilt of the turning planet.

Leaves transparent as dragonfly wings
fluttered in the breeze—dragonflies whose
compound eyes refracted summer sun.

Now it's gone to weed and seed, random
blossoms dropping petals, pesky volunteers
daring to poke their varied signatures up

through crumbling dirt. Sometimes children
come to play there, remembering faces in the
hearts of fallen flowers, seeking laughter in the

harsh caws of crows, or hiding in the tall grasses
that glitter gold in the slant rays of late afternoon.
But at night, for those who used to kneel beside

the flowerbeds, their spades turning fertile soil—
at night the garden blooms again, filling their
phantom arms with ghost bouquets as they

pass through one another—translucent spirits
haloed in faint moonlight, their fading faces
buried in the lingering scents of Earth.

For the Sycamore

I want to uncouple from the need to
squirrel memories in some deserted nest
high in the winter sycamore, the tree that
died last fall, was stripped of its limbs, cut
down to a stump, and ground to sawdust.

Tonight a ghostly sycamore groans in the
bitter New Year's wind, and withered roots
yearn to remember the blessing of rain.

Yet this tree leads to another—to another
sycamore I left behind on a corner lot of a
Cape Cod house, and to all those years of
leaves we raked to the curb, their great piles
hemming our yard until the leaf truck.

Its huge vacuum hose even sucked up our
dead cat Veronica one fall, shortly after a car
had ended her sweet and purring life.

I wanted this poem to begin anew, to turn
its back on Auld Lang Syne, but the squirrels
abandoned their nest weeks ago, leaving me
to fill it as I will with whatever I can find
and dig up to get me through the cold.

A Kind of Hunger

Where have they gone, those who stirred
the pancake batter, greased the pan for
the fish fry, shucked corn-on-the-cob,
sliced fresh tomatoes?

And where is the galvanized steel tub
we kids were sluiced in, salt and sand
running off our naked bodies as we
giggled, unashamed?

Night peers through the windows here,
casting shadows on the worn countertop,
the dulled stainless double-sink, the usual
dim and messy corner.

This kitchen breathes as if a sea-wind
has entered, riding the dark, sweeping
it all away until only hungry ghosts
remain, inhaling everything.

Honoring Angels

Angels enter dreams with warnings,
prophecies, orders from the Holy Spirit,
announce incarnations, even sometimes
raise those blessed by their presence into
the blazing habitat of God.

In a long ago dream one grabbed my hair
and swung me round and round as if we were
playing a child's game. I knew she would
soon let go, flinging me into the coral mist
surrounding us both, but I was afraid so woke
myself into a dark and empty room.

When an angel visits, should we hold on tight,
our mortal hand locked in her own, and let her
do with us as she will? Or should we wrestle him
to anchor in this world, beg for answers to
questions we can barely frame—demand
that he unmask and make us whole?

Undone

Undone, we yearn to wander off a path we know
onto another one—that beckoning animal trail
meandering into the undergrowth of twilight.

Twilight haunts us, hiding secrets in the density
of evergreens, burying them beneath ancient
boulders—notes from a visiting glacier's score.

Scores are everywhere, their notes begging
to be played by any instrument at hand, sung
by any creature who dares tongue.

Tongue, the strongest muscle in the body,
wants to stutter toward truth, until the teeth
clamp down, trapping the unspoken.

Unspoken, our tender wishes of the heart,
our fear of the unknown way, our reluctance
to risk going nowhere—and come out undone.

The Persistence of Ivy

I should have known that loss would feel
like this—ivy that invaded my childhood
bedroom windowsill finding me again

but flourishing now to fill the frame, filtering
day to dusk, the sun's faint rays threading its
tapestry like spider silk. My eyes have gone

greener still, competing with the evergreen
that screens my gaze as I search for you,
sure I will find you in this untamed garden.

I put on the old plaid shirt you wore, hoarding
the warmth of your remembered hand on my
frail shoulder. And I have put on my younger

face, cheeks flushed with anticipation, lips
slightly parted to taste again the shape of your
dear name. I know you will be in the pink of

health, don't want to greet you from the bench
I wait on, its iron fretwork cold on the back of
my thighs, but the ivy binds me here. Remember

our Carolina trip—roadside pecan trees hosting
mistletoe, billboards mute under kudzu? Please
don't tell me that we can't go home again.

Shadow World

It does not follow you like
the dependable companion
you've courted since childhood,

played hopscotch with, met in
a schoolyard jump-rope game,
or seen over your shoulder

dogging your steps in the sun
like a doppelganger flirting
with the several other selves

you might have been. It doesn't
stretch across the road, cast from
sunset in a tree, leaf shadows

quivering in the autumn wind,
leached of red and gold as they
receive their quantum twins.

But it lurks behind your eyes,
flickers in the dark of a village
on a map you haven't read yet,

luring you to trust and follow it
as if it were a summer solstice
sunrise cradled between stones.

Into the Lake

Gone now the fading pink plastic
drinking cup, slowly degrading at
the bottom of Lake Hopatcong,

the very cup Nana had used, the one
that lived on a wooden shelf below the
mirror above the pitted bathroom sink.

The cup was atop a laden paper bag,
and I accidentally knocked it from the raft
taking us and my newly grieving Poppy

to an island where the family cottage
nestled among dark pines. I lost the cup
overboard, and Poppy screamed.

His anguish echoes even now, a glissando
running up and down the keys of the
out-of-tune upright piano that sat in

the parlor of his brown-shingled house
on a tree-lined suburban street.
And in the house's ample pantry,

another pitted porcelain sink, and the
lingering scent of almost burnt toast
redeemed by cinnamon and liberal sugar.

Once, my husband and I revisited
that past. I mounted the peeling steps
to knock on the door, then peered into

the living-room window looking for Nana
and Poppy, for my mother, and for
the stained-glass window blessing

the landing at the foot of the stairs. Thank
God it was still there, still prisming sunlight
into radiant dust, but the rest had long gone

one-by-one into the lake, settling like years
of layered silt, though sometimes rising
to cloud the reedy bottom.

Whatever Fits

Whatever fits will be welcome.
William Stafford, from "Where We Are"

Years ago in a fifth grade classroom, I asked students
to write about objects I'd brought in: strangely striated
stones, broken tools, remnants of a bird's nest, a child's
knit mitten I'd found in the local thrift shop along with
the worn men's cashmere overcoat I'd remade to fit me.

I did not have the coat that day, but it swung in a black
and empty closet in my mind, not my closet but another's,
a closet storing nothing save the coat and a pair of galoshes—
the kind with snap-shut, black metal buckles, their toes
speckled with dust from another world.

Whatever fits will be welcome, the poet said. And as the
students wrote, I cupped my hands to heft the memory of
objects lost and found, all a good fit for their time. And I
intimately knew that overcoat, felt the old man wear it as
his only company, hang it nightly to guard his dreams.

I saw him leave the closet open so the streetlight slanting
through the blinds could warm the coat's familiar shoulders,
shine its buttons, even one hanging by a thread. I heard him
talking to the coat from the cave of his bed, knew he lived alone
somewhere on a street where it was always winter, and that he

often asked it, as I once heard my aging father ask my mother
in the middle of the night, *What's going to happen to us?*
I could not hear her murmured response from their bedroom
down the hall, but my father's question found the windows of
a row house in an invisible city, and an old coat answered it.

The Known Earth

Each winter my elderly neighbor's garden grew
oaktag stars, orange and yellow pointy things
painstakingly traced and cut by her trembling hands,
then mounted on sticks among dormant rose bushes.
After her death they flamed fiercely above the snow.

When the dead breathe their last, those atoms rise to
surround the known Earth as it rotates in place around
a black hole. The smoke from my father's cigarette
surrounded me as I lay full-length on the back seat
of Betsy-car, our1940s Chrysler sedan, staring at
the moon riding with us down some rural highway—
a familiar smoke that merged with the hypnotic hum
of the motor, the strobe of occasional streetlights.

Show me the way to go home,
I'm tired and I want to go to bed,

we'd sing as my father flicked butt after butt out
the car window. Those flickered like dying stars
along the road's edge, leaving in our wake tinder
for a field, sparks for a forest, and wads of paper
and shredded tobacco bleeding into sunrise.

My Father's Memory

He lost it, left it in the bottom
of the laundry basket, hidden
under dirty shorts, torn shirts.

He lost it in the bathroom
cabinet where the Tylenol lived—
couldn't open it to save his life.

He lost it in the pot he left
boiling on the stove, boiling
it dry as the tangled synapses

in his brain. He lost it, along with
his keys, in the sugar bowl, lost
it with the spare change hiding

under the used makeup in my
dead mother's bureau drawer,
powder coating everything.

He lost it in the television remote
he used to try to make a phone
call, and in the new car whose

buttons eluded his translation, so
he couldn't open its windows and
locked doors and panicked until

he wet himself. And he lost it when
he yelled *Shut the fuck up* at his
daughter who only wanted him to

come to the table and celebrate
her birthday; to enjoy fried chicken
homemade potato salad, and cake.

Later in the ER on the day he died,
he kept asking who would pay for
this since he hadn't yet lost the words

for money although he couldn't
remember our names. He lost it,
lost it, lost it . . . end of story.

Houses

The first one I constructed grew from the
white cardboard pieces hiding inside my
father's starched shirts. I slipped these out,
cut them down for walls, bent and taped
them together to make the whole house,
then put it on the floor of my room.

There were little cardboard tables and chairs,
tiny beds with cotton-ball pillows and napkin
blankets. Then came the paper-doll family who
would live there—mother, father, children,
and small brown dog—all these brought to
life from my Crayola box of colors.

Lying on my stomach and hanging off the side
of my bed, I hovered over my creation,
maneuvering little people from one room
to another, bringing them dawn and dusk,
breakfast and dinner. Laughter and tears
rounded the corners of their given days.

Decades later, my granddaughter played dolls
in the carefully constructed house her grandfather
made her, its shingled roof and painted rooms
a showplace, the tiny beds so real I wanted to
shrink and lie down in one. Now it gathers dust
in a corner of my daughter's guest room.

Count up all the houses—all we've dreamed
or lived in. Like children at play we make them,
believe in them, people them with family and friends.
And they remember us—windows open, doors
unlocked and swinging in the wind. They call us
to stop by, and sometimes—sometimes we do.

Remember Me?

Remember me? I am the abandoned house
you dream about, the farmhouse whose
ample porch holds a row of rocking chairs.

Days, I nap by the creek in whose blue eye
my deep reflection shimmers. You have visited
me many nights, even braved my underwater
rooms where a family of dreamers gathers.

They, too, know you, have come like you
in every season to drift from room to room,
greeting one another in glad recognition.

The wind brings me news of a place called city
where dwellings live atop one another. Wind says
dreamers who go there enter cyclones of desire.
But for you—my fertile fields and peaceful waters.

Listening to Furniture

Were things otherwise, I would not be listening
to furniture in the rooms of my head.
I would leave the old couch in the living-room
just as it is—cherish the dented cushion where
you sit day after day, and the back pillow whose
top seams slide downward from the weight of
your shoulders and sleeping head.

Were things otherwise, the stack of fake logs
by the fireplace would never be used, but huddle
there forever, waiting for the next polar freeze,
and the corner rocking chair would still be sitting
motionless by the window.

And what about the small dining table with its loose
legs, all four a bit wobbly like my own? Were things
otherwise, it would stand there forever, shaky but
proud, along with its four maple chairs, its surface
littered with vitamin bottles, papers, and crumbs.

Fluff me up, begs the couch. *Burn me,* hiss the logs.
*For the love of God, clean me off and tighten my
screws so I can be foursquare,* whines the table. *Please
help me rock the night away,* the rocking chair whimpers,
moonlight trapped between its white spindles.

Far from home, I heed the supplications of the lonely,
feel the pain of the neglected, then do what I can.

Freeze-Frames

When I pull the steaks from the freezer,
part the wax paper between them, finger
the frost marbling the paper, the fat marbling
the meat, they become alien, the microscope
of the familiar suddenly spiraling away.

I become the inspector of the anonymous
as I tap frozen slabs against the black marble
counter-top where they will thaw, or stare into
my stainless sink, an undiscovered wilderness
that beckons me.

Now I contemplate the aging cast iron skillet on
the big electric burner, a pan that may have sat
over a campfire sizzling a fresh-caught bluefish
whose bones were lifted out and tossed aside
into a litter of decaying leaves.

Steak in one life, fish in another—all freeze-frames,
and we wander through the pixels, stopping now
and then to join the stills—asking these familiar
strangers to call our name, to lead us back into
the communal kitchen, the ongoing feast.

Breaking Morning

Waking, you look at the clock.
Not yet sunrise, but you know
morning is breaking over the sill
of your still blinded window.
You yawn and stretch,

remembering last summer's waves
breaking against your side while
your planted feet kept sinking
into sand, little swales forming
around them as if the sea floor

would swallow you. Soon light is
seeping under the blinds, waves and
particles falling from our local star,
and somewhere a farmer gathers
fresh eggs for your breaking.

Last one in is a rotten egg!

And last one up is, too, you think,
as you levitate from the bed, swim
through the chilly air toward the
bathroom, fill the sink with hot
water, and bend to wash your face.

Seeing Familiar Faces

It happens often, this seeing familiar
faces on passers-by, sometimes spanning
time and place, as when a friend's face
suddenly shifts from youth to age,
then back to your mutual now.

Sometimes it's our own face we see
reflected in another, a certain slant
of the eyes, tilt of the chin, angle of
a glance that meets ours, then shifts
back to join its own parade.

After my husband died, in dreams that grew
less frequent over time, I saw his face receding,
washing away into light. No dream mirror to
show me who I had become, no blind hands
reaching out to teach me my own features.

It is all one—calcium blooming into a nose,
shaping cheekbones, sockets for the eyes.
The faces we seek are those we want to love
or be loved by, even that stranger on whom
we are suddenly spilling the story of our life.

II

Beyond the Mirror

In the ICU you ask me to bring you
a mirror. I think you want to see
your face—thinning hair, sparse beard,
and cheeks almost as pale as the pillow
cradling your head.

I fear bringing you one, believe you
will despair as the mirror confirms
that you are dying—confirms that
fact for both of us, although the doctor
still is dangling hope.

It's like Star Trek in here, you say,
you know, the Sick Bay, as you
stare at the TV above your bed, the one
showing the Theraflu commercial where
a woman takes a spoonful and pinks up.

When I bring you the mirror, you only
gaze briefly at your face, then angle it
to reflect the single window behind your
bed, the one that opens onto red maples
and a deep autumn sky.

And I understand that you need to know
the world is still there, though you sense
you will be leaving it; want to rise above
your body and know where you are
before the mirror dies.

A New Beginning

A new beginning is what we hoped for
that day in the hospital when the massage
therapist gave him a comforting shoulder rub—
that day when we did not yet know.

His hair had grown to brush the collar of
his hospital gown, and I remember tugging
at those curls, loving the thick white waves
that flowed from brow to nape.

He didn't want the haircut on the menu
of services. Perhaps, somehow, he sensed
what was to come. We thought that we had
promises to keep, although we all must walk

the long good-bye. I've heard that both
the one who goes and the one who follows
must find the portal to a new beginning.
I loved him into death and then beyond.

Love is a long hello. An aging widow in my
grief group who dares to say she wants to
love again, who always brings her bottle of
non-alcoholic wine to the communal supper

after meetings, raises her glass to desire
although sometimes she grows silent,
gazing into the unmapped landscape of
the white tablecloth.

They're Coming Back

They're coming back, the man in the nursing home
told my friend about their recently dead wives.
Really! Mine's coming back, and so is your wife.

Mine's gonna appear right here at my room door.
Yours gonna be home when you get there. Have faith.
They're coming back. You know it, and so do I!

Soon it will be the holidays, holy-days, painful
lonely days—an empty chair yawning at the head
of the formerly festive dinner table.

Who will make the perfect gravy or bake this year's
apple pie or cake, steaming cinnamon and sugar?
Who will carve the turkey, the ham, the roast?

This morning a woman in our grief support group
just lost her second husband. Risky to care again.
Scary to have opened a scarred heart again.

Out there the autumn trees have finally begun
to turn, scarlet and gold arcing over the road—
stained glass cathedrals embracing sunlight.

Anniversary

Oh aching day go choke
on your familiar tune

that endless replay of
the strata of our loss.

Your orbit is a curse
a comet spewing ice,

your annual return
predictable as rust.

Catch a passing freight
or hitchhike down the pike,

the wake of your exhaust
dead weeds along the way.

Go find another home
and sink a garden there,

feed funeral bouquets
for mourners everywhere.

No scent of roses done
or blood from sudden thorn

can thrust me into arms
that once again are gone.

Valentine's Day at the Spousal Loss Support Group

One by one, they straggle in, some bringing
heart-shaped boxes of candy to give the rest,
others with simple Valentines bearing heartfelt
notes of thanks to the group for mutual support.

And then she enters, a bit late, a box of
gooey donuts in her hand, their garish icing
gleaming through the cellophane box lid—
more than enough for all.

Widowed now for two years, she's brought
a variety—some iced with sticky chocolate,
some neon pink, and some glazed vanilla
topped with multi-colored sprinkles.

She's sorry she was late, but she stopped
to pick them up on her way because it's
Valentine's Day, her husband was a cop, and
they always had donuts down at the station.

We pass the box around, carefully lift out our
choices, placing them on the red napkins
she's also thought to bring. We always go out
to lunch after meetings, and many of us

shouldn't be eating this much sugar, or don't
really like such rich and gooey treats, but we
eat them together while sharing our memories,
tempering the bitter with the sweet.

Because the Duck

She kept many animals—dogs,
goats, chickens, and the duck—
the duck her late husband had
named, held in his arms and
loved especially.

She kept many animals, but
the duck meant the most since
it was his duck, he'd loved it
especially, and what he'd loved
she loved the best.

This morning she went out
to feed the duck and found it
headless, head ripped off by
some kind of raptor, swooping
in for a horrible kill!

Sobbing to me on the phone
she said the neighbor lost two
turkeys the same way last night,
but losing her husband's duck
felt like she'd lost *him* again.

It will never be the same because
the raptor keeps circling, waiting to
dive and grab her head with its cruel
claws, then sink its beak deep into
her skull because the duck . . .

To Ride the Waves

We vowed to ride the waves
and not go under after, on our honeymoon,
you swam out beyond the breakers
      until the rip tide carried you too far, and
            the lifeguard rose to stand on his chair.

We vowed to ride the waves toward shore,
never to venture too far out again, never again
to see our heads like small black dots, distant
      bits of flotsam or jetsam—
            punctuation marks in the long story

of the sea. He told me he was a strong
swimmer, vowed he could hold his own against
any tide, but he was wrong, and though
      he made it back to shore that day,
            another fiercer tide took him away,

across the bar, beyond the skill of any guard on
sea or land. We vowed before the altar to be true
until death do us part, and kept that vow,
      but now he floats, not dead man's but
            beyond all reach while I still ride the waves.

Marmalade

Sitting in our regular booth in the Prestige Diner,
often on our way home from some poetry event
or other, you always ordered eggs over-easy
and whole wheat toast, but we could never find
those little plastic packets of orange marmalade
in the small square dish by the napkin holder.

Now that you're dead, do you still love marmalade?
Before we knew you were sick, we were driving
through a spring landscape, branches blossoming
white, sweet and easy miles disappearing beneath
our quiet tires, when suddenly you said,
I can't imagine all this going on without me!

How fluently the names forsythia, red maple
flowed from our tongues that day, the engine
of our life together well-tuned and fuel efficient.
How can it be eight years since you drove alone
over the horizon? Yet I, too, have moved on,
weathered lonely nights, betrayals of my own body.

There is still marmalade, the sticky jar on my shelf
almost empty. I spread it thickly on this morning's
whole wheat toast, and its bitter sugar lingers
on my aging tongue. Dearest, wherever you are,
know the heart makes room for other loves, although
I love you still, and I wish you marmalade on toast.

Two Meteors

Two meteors flared last night, flamed above
the twilit trees, their arcing signatures dropping
so quickly they sputtered out and died.

Driving on, I thought that we must burn through
whatever sorrows ride our shoulders, or learn to
carry them like that young turtle I saw today

crossing the road before me, bearing his shell.
I did not stop to help, only swerved to avoid him,
then looked in the rear-view mirror, hoping that

he was still on his way. And I wrapped a prayer
around his fragile back, blessing his stumpy legs
and plodding faith on that slowly darkening road.

Across the Autumn Field

Who comes across the autumn field, bearing
an armful of dry corn stalks like a woman
might hold an infant, cradling them in the
slant light that cloaks his hunched shoulders?

And why is he walking toward you, his
work shoes sinking into the dust, while you,
barefoot and rooted, a leafless sapling at the
field's edge, can only wait to receive his gift?

Behind him, a mule pulls a harrower, erasing
his path, breaking the soil to render it fertile,
turning dry clods over to ready them for
storm clouds now billowing on the horizon.

Beyond the field is a woods, and at its center
a plot for green burial, and suddenly you know
that the approaching stranger only wants to
welcome you, hand you his spent stalks with

their story, their knowing that what enters
the earth will emerge again, green and tender,
and that the sapling you have become will
flourish new leaves when the rains arrive.

Autumn Walk

I am not thinking about you as I pass
the neighbor's white trumpet flowers,
sagging as they spill from the vine—
so tenderly cared for before her death.

Nor am I thinking of you when the sun-
dappled leaves cast their shadows on the
rough macadam, their high rustling like
a fall of glitter spangling my bare arms.

The nearby tidal brook is low, its surface
a veil of scum. *Keep Out,* the sign says, but
I can feel the turtles and small fish going
about their lives, hidden in brackish water.

And now by the ball field, where the sky
opens, and the horizon darkens with trees,
I count my loves as if they are candles on
a birthday cake—and do not blow them out.

Butterfly Kisses

The Butterfly Effect: According to quantum theory, a hurricane in China can be caused by a butterfly flapping its wings on the other side of the planet. If the butterfly had not flapped its wings at just the right point in space/time, the hurricane would not have happened.

When I visited my Nana's house,
she'd tuck me in and kiss me
goodnight with butterfly kisses—
delicately merging her eyelashes
with mine as we blinked together.

Years later, I butterfly-kissed my own
children to sleep, bent over them
mingling my eyelashes with theirs,
or sometimes just grazing their cheeks
with a faint tickling.

Lovers, husbands have come and gone
over the years, some welcoming my gift
of butterfly-kisses, others shying away.
Once I saw a migrating Monarch cover
another with its wings, becoming one.

If there is a heaven, if the tiny breeze
born from the opening and closing
of our eyelids with those of the beloved
can find its way there, what angel might
open its wingspan to enfold us?

Spring Blues

The thicket grown tall in the pasture
where the horses used to be glitters
in the late afternoon sun, leans toward
the field halfway down the mountainside,
now turning rosy in slant rays.

Soon shadows descend on thicket and field
and a blue wind sweeps in from the distant
ridge. Trees moan in that wind, their roots
calling one another beneath cold soil, while
budding leaves whisper green birth.

In the photo on my wall, a single fox stands
at the edge of a rock-strewn field, head lifted,
ears alert to whatever small rustling might flash
among the wild grasses. Last night, as the blue
wind coursed in my window, I *was* that fox,

nostrils flaring, head tilted toward the sky,
inhaling snow melt chill from the Milky Way
as bright cold gilded my cheeks. And later, in
my dreams, old lovers came to visit, new ones
lay down in sleep beside me, and it was spring.

The Eastern Bluebird on Spring Grass

On this spring equinox, a bluebird flits from
newly green to yellow grasses, flashes a rosy
breast, then flies to the fencepost.

I think of you, husband—how every Easter
afternoon before we were together you went
in search of Eastre, pagan goddess of spring,

tramping out into woods or fields, looking
for her signs. *Fly here to my window,* I silently
ask the bluebird, your talisman of rebirth,

bring me birdsong from the dead. All night
I listened to sleet pinging outside my open
window, pulled aside the curtains in the gray

pre-dawn light to see glistening pebbles and the
silver slope of the lawn. Yet this morning every
blade of grass, every bud slipping yellow from its

green stem tells me that tonight's full moon will
scatter brilliant light above the clouds while the
bluebird, nestled on her eggs, will warm us all.

Measuring the Distance

Unroll a tape measure, stretch it
across the fabric of a day, a year.
Record the reach of the wind
or the height of corn stalks
greening in an abandoned field.

If your tape be infinite, you will
never see the end of it; if finite,
you will run out of numbers,
and clock hands will cease
their commentary.

Raise your two hands before you,
palms facing, and feel the tension
between them as you expand and
compress the invisible accordion
of your days.

Then try to measure love—love
that can leap any distance to fuse
your atoms with those of your
beloved until you resonate together,
harmonics pure as a tuning fork.

Darning Socks

The hole usually wears in the heel
after the wool has thinned, so that
held against the morning, one sees
a patchwork, a woven crossing
of strands. And then the hole

appears, calling for needle and yarn,
for stitches to be made around the
circle or tear, then criss-crossed back
and forth to weave endurance, to patch
what can last for a little longer.

Wounds after surgery are often closed
with staples, or glued against chance
opening. Inner wounds are stitched
by skilled surgeons whose hands
have practiced darning flesh.

Whether socks or mortal meat be
mended, held up to either sun or moon
the sky will break through, haloing
the edges of all wounds, then sealing
them with light.

Healing the Wound with Honey

Numerous studies have shown that difficult-to-heal wounds respond well to honey dressings.

It must have been inflicted in another life,
this wound we can't remember, not even sure
whose it may have been. Sometimes we feel
a rift in the flesh needing stitches, or a wound

of the spirit that even the heavy blue dressing
of the sky can't fix—an invisible fissure in the
heart or brain, cradled in our arms like a refugee
child too damaged to weep.
.

Sometimes we hear the bees whose sting is less
important than their task of filling the comb
for the queen, or the beekeeper in his white suit
and gloves, humming back at the hive.

We each have a job to do—the bees to gather
nectar and transform it into honey, the beekeeper
to steal the pot of gold. And what is our work,
we who need to learn the art of scars?

We must learn the names of honey, give its
sticky sweetness to our tongues, fill our
cupped hands with healing, and offer it to the
ancestors of our still open wounds.

When I Taught Her How to Tie Her Shoes

A revelation, the student
in high school who didn't know
how to tie her shoes.

I took her into the book-room, knowing
what I needed to teach was perhaps more
important than Shakespeare or grammar,

guided her hands through the looping,
the pulling of the ends. After several
tries, she got it, walked out the door

empowered. How many lessons are like
that—skills never mastered in childhood,
simple tasks ignored, let go for years?

This morning, my head bald from chemotherapy,
my feet farther away than they used to be
as I bend to my own shoes, that student

returns to teach me the meaning of life:
to simply tie the laces and walk out
of myself into this sunny winter day.

Dream Hat

Someone tossed a hat into the sky,
flicked it with one hand like a frisbee.

Look, it's still traveling, spiraling off
into the ever-more, never again to be

head-bound. Is it the soft little cloche
I wore during last winter's chemotherapy,

nestling over my bald scalp and cold ears?
Or the straw sunhat whose woven brim

I wound bright scarves around, flinging
spring flowers into the face of infusions?

Or perhaps it is the hand-knit cap I wore
as a baby, the one immortalized in the old

black album, the one where I'm sitting up
in my carriage, waving hello to this world.

On Pike's Peak I Eat Donuts

I did it! Made it to the top of Pike's Peak,
elevation over fourteen-thousand feet!
Last time I was high in the Rockies
at a Continental Divide four-thousand feet
lower, I could hardly breathe, felt dizzy—
fluid compressing my heart from a cancer
I didn't yet know was stalking me.

But this time, atop Pike's Peak, the cold
wind blowing me sideways, the air so thin
that when I walk fast my ribs ache from
sucking it in, I eat donuts, deep fried
donuts, crunchy brown donuts, hot donuts
so moist my fingers drip, and the napkins
wrapped around them turn to gold.

The famous Pike's Peak Donuts, so sweet
in my mouth, so good, I had to order more,
clutching the greasy bag all the long way
down, savoring the taste of health around
every switchback—each succulent bite
saying, *You've done it, girl! You've done it,
climbed above the tree line and come back.*

Running Wild

The great clock of your life is slowing down,
and the small clocks run wild.
                                        Stanley Kunitz

I am running again through the woods next to
my childhood yard, my small legs dodging fallen
branches, thick brambles, maybe even poison ivy,
as I gallop through some summer's sticky heat.

I am running like our small beagle Berry,
named for wild blackberries, who dashed
headlong into a tree upon our return from
a treeless, sun-blind shore—and lived.

I am running wild although it's darker now
here in this new time zone where the hours
grow hallow beneath the mirror of the moon—
a moon inching further from the Earth each year.

A great clock ticks on the horizon, but small clocks
pulse within me, giddy with urgency, as I dodge
trees and leap streams, trusting my feet to find
firm ground beneath the flickering stars.

The Great North Woods

Not sure when it began, this growing
ache for woods although daily I drive
between patches of scrub oaks and
pines that do well in sandy soil.

Faintly, I hear the woods that sang
at night on the winds of childhood,
soughing outside my bedroom windows
every season, even in winter when snow

linked the trees like their wandering
network of roots. Many days I followed
deer prints in the creek, or animal paths
in and out of thorny tangles.

The Great North Woods haunted my
dreams, and I entered them, seeking
again the little cottage whose windows
welcomed me with candles—who waited

for me to open the door to a fire in the
hearth, a pot of hot soup, and a gentle dog
whose paws trembled as it chased dream
rabbits among the shivering pines.

A Prayer the Body Makes

In fetal position, our knees drawn up,
arms parallel in supplication, and eyes

rolled back into the skull of sleep,
that dark absence that swallows us,

wrapping us in ivy, evergreen from
birth to death. A prayer the body makes

beyond words, beyond the unheard
frequencies of cells broadcasting into

the abyss, beyond the arc of another
body curling warm against our own,

belly rising, falling. *Translate,* the mind
demands. *Translate this prayer that we*

may all practice it together. Translate the
body's pores breathing in, breathing out,

breathing in, breathing out—asleep or
awake—in the wordless center holding all.

The Solitary Birch

The solitary birch in the center
of the greening field by the train tracks
stretches slender bare limbs skyward

as if it were a woman transformed
after forbidden union with a god—
rooted there forever.

Over time, she will forget having
been mortal, will forget her longing
for the family of tree, will learn to

expect nothing more than the budding
of new leaves, the heat of summer sun,
the autumn winds of quivering gold,

and winter's letting go. On the horizon
ancient ones watch her—mountains purple
in the coming dusk. At field's edge,

a stream disappears into the undergrowth,
carrying last light toward the darkening
center of an old growth woods.

Now the train we are on carries us into
the landscape of night, whistling past
flashing red lights at the crossings.

The birch is long gone, yet it lingers
glimmering white as bone, learning
to expect nothing, not even itself.

Three Lives

1.

To enter marriage at twenty, old enough
and yet too young, too young.

Old enough to cook mushrooms and peas
to mix into rice, too young to understand
the landlady downstairs is dying, even
as she feeds raw hamburger to the spaniel
nesting on her lap.

And oh the joy of listening to curfew bells
chiming across the river, delighted to be
out of the confines of dormitory life.

Old enough to bring a baby boy
home to a used crib in the living room
after twenty hours hard labor.

2.

To finally decide to divorce, after
the first house, years of holiday meals,
barbecues, two children, and a series
of dogs—the last one that chewed the
window frames left behind.

After predictable chimes from the alarm
meaning time to get up for another day
escaping the confines of four walls, of
one closet with both his and her clothes.

Old enough to know the sorrow of losing
what might have been, yet still too young
to know the gift of looking back with
forgiveness, another kind of love.

3.

To dare to love again, marry again—
so many lives we leave behind—
now cooking vegetarian, sharing the
daily red pot of tea, driving nights to
lofts in Manhattan where poems chime.

Still too young to believe death
is moving closer, cancer a promise
on the horizon, and then, and then . . .

In the ICU after savoring lemon sorbet
melting on his tongue, he gives me his
wedding ring, makes his peace with our
goodbye, dies while I sing *Amazing Grace,*

and I am old enough to know this incantation
is a newborn child I bring home to myself.

Whose Newborn

Whose newborn has surfaced in my dream
toward waking? And where is her mother?
I bend over her bassinet, coo at her,
peer into her eyes—piercing blue with
occasional clouds wandering through.

Today the sky is brilliant, the mountains
a red rock cradle for the weight of all that
indigo. Ravens spiral above some riddle
dead among the sagebrush, and their
hoarse cries echo on the morning wind.

A baby born with the sky in her eyes,
cumulus meandering by—may she
be healthy, may she be strong as the
mountain, clear as the stream that
carves the canyon. May she be me.

About the Author

Penny Harter lives in Mays Landing, NJ. Her poems have been published widely in journals and anthologies, and her literary autobiography appears as an extended essay in *Contemporary Authors Autobiography Series, Volume 28* (1998) as well as in *Contemporary Authors, Volume 172* (1999). A poem of hers was featured in *American Life in Poetry,* and journals such as *Persimmon Tree, Rattle, Tattoo Highway, Tiferet,* and *Windhover* have published her work.

Recent poems appear in the anthologies *Poetry of Presence, The Book of Donuts,* and *Healing the Divide.* Her essays and poems also appear in the writing guides *Wingbeats: Exercises & Practice in Poetry, The Crafty Poet: A Portable Workshop, The Crafty Poet II,* and *The Practice of Poetry.*

Her most recent books include *The Resonance Around Us, One Bowl, Recycling Starlight,* and *The Night Marsh.* With her late husband William J. Higginson, she co-authored *The Haiku Handbook* (25th Anniversary Edition, 2010).

Harter was a featured reader at the 2010 Geraldine R. Dodge Poetry Festival, and she has won three poetry fellowships from the New Jersey State Council on the Arts, an award from the Geraldine R. Dodge Foundation, the Mary Carolyn Davies Award from the Poetry Society of America, the first William O. Douglas Nature Writing Award for her work in *American Nature Writing,* 2002, and two residencies from Virginia Center for the Creative Arts.

Made in the USA
Monee, IL
11 November 2020

47256873R00049